The
MYSTERIOUS LADY
OF THE MOOR
by Judy Chard

Beatrice Chase - John Oxenham's

"MY LADY OF THE MOOR"

First published 1994 by
Orchard Publications
2 Orchard Close, Chudleigh, Newton Abbot, Devon TQ13 0LR.
Telephone (0626) 852714

ORCHARD
PUBLICATIONS

ISBN 1 898964 04 1

Typeset and printed by Swift Print, Dawlish, Devon

ACKNOWLEDGEMENTS

I should like to express my gratitude to the people who have written and talked to me as mentioned in my foreword, shown me letters and lent me photographs, and to the Longman Group UK Ltd for giving me permission to quote from *"Through a Dartmoor Window"* by Beatrice Chase published by them in 1915. This includes 1,400 words from the text for which they are making no charge and which covers the Commonwealth and the USA Market in the English language.

Photographs: *Cover and Back Cover of Beatrice Chase,*
Page 9, 21, 29, 34 - Miss Enid Shortbridge.
Cover Transparency of Dartmoor - Phil Eldridge
Others are by the author.

Author's Foreword

It was with some trepidation that at the request of Orchard Publications I wrote this book on Beatrice Chase for tens of thousands of words have already been written about this fascinating character.

I have read most of her books and John Oxenham's extraordinary novel in which he made her his heroine - *"My Lady of the Moor."*

In my signed copy of *"Through a Dartmoor Window"* is pasted a cutting from a local newspaper of the 1930s giving the details of an interview with Beatrice and with this I decided to open my book as it is a typical newspaper description of her. But I was fortunate in that I had a great deal of material which had not been published before, in fact is unique, both letters and photographs, and it was on these I based the second half of the book.

Mr George Train of Teignmouth had written me a long letter after he had read my book *"About Widecombe"* in which he wrote of Beatrice whom he had known well; Miss Enid Shortbridge to whom I talked, had been a close friend of Beatrice for 30 years, Mr and Mrs Fred Miners of Ashburton had rented a cottage from her in the 1940s, Peter Hicks of Venton Farm was another of the people who knew her well as he lived at Venton Farm during her lifetime and she left it to him in her will.

I had a feeling that these people would give me a clearer insight into the real Beatrice Chase or Katharine Parr, which was her real name. Whether this is so you must judge for yourself, to me she is still 'The Mysterious Lady of the Moor'.

Finally, before I get irate letters regarding the spelling of "Cobley", I have used the form which has been offered by whomsoever gave me the information, although "Cobley" is the usual Devonian form, not Cobleigh.

Also many people write and talk of "Kitty" Jay's grave but Enid, among many others, insist her name was "Mary" Jay.

I hope you enjoy reading the book as much as I did writing it.

Judy Chard, Morley Farm. March 1994

The Mysterious Lady Of The Moor
Beatrice Chase

"So this is England at the present - no wonder the best citizens emigrate!"
Those words were uttered by the writer, Beatrice Chase over four
decades ago. They could well have been spoken today and in many ways
she was ahead of her time, both mentally and physically. She believed in
sunshine, fresh air and orange juice – the cure for all ills. How she would
have loved today's Health Shops.

She had good reason for these beliefs for she had developed t.b. at the
age of 28 when she and her mother were living in London and they both
worked tirelessly in the slums and workhouses where the disease was
rampant.

Born in 1874 at Harrow in Middlesex, the eldest child of Mr Charles
Parr, she was educated at the convent of the Holy Child in Cavendish
Square. The family came from Kendal Castle in Westmorland and her real
name was Olive Katharine Parr, Beatrice Chase the pen name she chose.

She was a descendent of William Parr, brother of Katharine, wife of
Henry VIII and with a nice touch of irony, when she was accused of having
a bad temper she would say – "I have a dash of Tudor blood which
accounts for it." Because of this ancestry she wore a signet ring with the
seal of the Rose of Lancaster engraved on it, and it is true she did resemble
her ancestor with the same red gold hair and blue eyes.

Among her other forebears were the Knights of the Golden Fleece and
those of the Saint Esprit.

She and her mother came to Venton House near Widecombe on
Dartmoor at the turn of the century as the doctor had told her the moorland
air would cure her complaint, which proved to be true.

Perhaps in view of the comments she had made it is as well she is not alive today in a world which would be even more inexplicable and unacceptable to the Lady of the Moor, than it was even then. This name was given to her by fellow writer John Oxenham, who wrote a book about her naming her Lady of the Moor, the intensity of his admiration being something of an embarrassment to Beatrice. It was the death in action of her fiancé in the first world war, a shock from which she never recovered, which made her Faith and her work her interest and consolation and one of her interests was the Crusade for Chastity which she originated. However to some people she did appear imperious and awe inspiring, whilst to others, easy of approach and sympathetic.

Perhaps for the fastidious her writing was a little too luscious and extravagant, but both her fiction and non-fiction about Dartmoor appealed

Venton House Extension

Venton Farm

to an enormous variety of people world-wide and she believed passionately in herself and her work.

She was bitterly opposed to the National Parks Scheme and the use of the moor by the military being keen on preservation of the status quo and it was her writing about the beauties of Dartmoor which made her the darling of the reading public during that period before and during the first world war.

Many writers had been, and still are, inspired by Dartmoor as the plethora of books which fill the shops proves, but as an ex journalist she could to some extent write in a detached manner of its beauty, its legends and folklore in a semi-reporting style, telling the truth without exaggerated and imaginative embellishments which had so often been the case in the past.

She wrote brilliant pen portraits of farmers and their families, of such local people as Thirza Endacott, who tried to kill herself because she thought a curse had been put on her by a witch – of Grannie Caunter who bore one of the most common names in the area, you only have to visit the churchyard at Widecombe to see the number of Caunters who rest there.

There was the man who had been injured by a shot gun when out shooting rabbits, he had to wear a mask much like the Phantom of the Opera to hide his ravaged face.

Her servant, Mr Bluejacket appears in many of her books, an ex naval man who kept the house shipshape and Bristol fashion. He waited at the table, and did all the housework for Beatrice and her mother – far better than the girls she had employed before, to whom she referred as having been "half witted and incompetent."

In my particular signed copy of *"Through a Dartmoor Window"*, the follow up to her best seller, *"The Heart of the Moor"*, is pasted a cutting of an interview written in the late 1930s for a local paper. It gives such a clear portrait of the writer in her heyday that I quote it in full.

"I found a legend but a day ago right in the heart of Widecombe, a woman with copper gold hair and vivid blue eyes for whom Knights rode bravely into battle not so very long ago.

Thousands rallied to the call of Miss Beatrice Chase during the Great War and in her tiny chapel in Widecombe you will find the "White Crusaders" Roll of Honour. Her knights went bravely into battle knowing that in England there was one who prayed always for their safe return. It was from one of them Miss Chase received her most treasured possession, a Heavenly Cross set with twelve stones from the Heavenly City.

The famous authoress (in real life Miss Katharine Parr) brought her beloved jewel for my inspection. "It was given me by a grandson of the late Duke of Buccleuch and a cousin of our present Queen," she said simply "A priceless treasure. It is probably the only one in the world, even in the Vatican I do not think there is another like it."

TWENTY YEARS WAIT

Jasper, sapphire, chalcedony, emerald, sardonyx, sardius, chrysalite, beryl, topaz, chrysoprase, jacinth – the twelfth an amethyst – a round eye of each twinkles from the cross. Thus when Miss Chase wrote her last and most famous book she called it *"The Twelfth An Amethyst."*

"I have never written since. I waited twenty years to write that book. I knew when it was done that it was my best and so I laid my pen away." she told me. She still toyed with her cross. The heavy gold chain from which it hung was specially made in India, each link of dull gold bearing on its surface 33 polished stars, symbolic of the stars of heaven. "There are 2,200 stars altogether, see how they twinkle, almost like gems," said Miss Chase, twisting them against the light.

There are many treasures in this chapel. Brilliant sunshine filtering through the lovely stained glass windows lit up a Military Cross, war medals and regimental badges given their leader by Knights of the White Crusade. It was after a safe return from Vimy Ridge that Miss Chase was given the Military Cross and DSO by one of them Miss Chase said with a reminiscent smile.

MANY PILGRIMS

Over 300 people visit this little chapel daily during the summer months. They may wonder why the Rose of Lancaster is so often seen within the chapel. You will see it on the silver lamp which burns so steadily near the altar, and again on the cup of a lovely silver chalice and in the stained glass window. It is part of Miss Chase's family crest.

Miss Chase pointed to the lamp which shed a clear red glow upon our upturned faces. "I burn that for the sick, often for people I have never met in my life," she said, "People send me telegrams sometimes, asking me to burn my lamp for a sick friend and it has seemed sometimes as though it has brought people back to life.

Long ago there was another Katharine Parr and for her beautiful golden hair, clear milk and roses complexion, and bright blue eyes, Henry VIII

The chapel today

chose her as his queen. It was Katharine who survived him and lived to marry again. From her brother, William Parr, sprang Miss Chase's ancestors. The authoress finds it interesting to recall that since that day, our present Queen Elizabeth is England's first commoner queen.

We left the chapel and Miss Chase showed me her tiny garden with its sun corner. We sat a while in the gaily striped chairs. "Now you can swagger and say you have sat in Dartmoor sun on a winter's day," she laughed.

AWAKES AT 5 AM

The garden is another delight of this energetic woman, and she tends her flowers and seedlings carefully. So full are her days that she rises each day at 5 am. "I could never cope with all my letters and housework otherwise," she told me. Then she chuckled. There is something infectious about that chuckle. "Doctors say no self respecting microbe would live with me you know. I have a cold bath every day when I get up, and do exercises for twenty minutes too."

Each morning the postman trudges up the little hill which bears upon its brow the quaint 16th century cottage which is Miss Chase's home. Letters for 'Venton' are always numerous, and it takes Miss Chase several hours each day to answer them.

Miss Chase's correspondents live in all parts of the world and write for advice on all kinds of problems.

But I have not told you of the authoress's most constant companions. Peter the Pooh is a dignified tortoise-shell cat and his nephew, Tim is almost equally beloved of his mistress.

Blazing open fires welcomed us to the cottage again, and in Angel Corner we spent the remainder of the afternoon. It is here that Miss Chase wrote her books.

All the rooms in the house are named. There is the Shadow Room, the Sunshine Room, the Rainbow Maker's corner, but of these I must tell you another day. For a while we must say au revoir to the "Lady of the Moor."

~oOo~

In this copy of *"Through a Dartmoor Window"*, under the heading "A Silver Jubilee" is written as a foreword...

"Miss Beatrice Chase who is widely known by her contributions to literature, is this week celebrating the 25th anniversary of the day when she left London to take up residence in Devon. The change is one on which she is to be felicitated. It was evidently to her liking for she has never thought of going back. At Widecombe-in-the-Moor where she lives, she is as much at home as Uncle Tom Cobleigh himself. No wise visitor to that charming rural retreat misses the opportunity if it presents itself, of making her acquaintance and seeing something of the treasures she has gathered about her at Venton House. Devon is to be congratulated on having gained a good neighbour, and one who thoroughly appreciates the advantages of living in the West. It will be hoped she will live to celebrate the golden jubilee of her migration and continue to enjoy the benefit she has found in it."

Western Morning News

2nd February 1934.

From *"The Globe"* of Toronto.

"The only writer who has mystically interpreted Dartmoor. A descendent of the family of the sixth wife of Henry VIII. Beatrice Chase's own name is Olive Katharine Parr. Under the two names she has written thirty volumes and many magazine articles ... the home on the moor she seldom leaves, but lives and works here in the surroundings she loves and among the people whose joys and sorrows are here".

Beatrice herself wrote an author's note in this book...

"I am warned by reviewers and others to have no plot in this book. It is amazing how frequently during the past year, the average reader, especially the woman reader, has said to me 'If only you Dartmoor writers would leave out the plots and give us just the moor and your daily life and the people.' I feel strongly that the reading public has the right to demand the style of the book it wishes to read. We writers are, or ought to be, the servants of the public and in a letter from Jeremy who in his wisdom wrote to me (the letter made me unreasonably and ungratefully angry) 'Never mind the plot. People can get plots from the gutter press, the Police News, and the divorce court, what men want is atmosphere. Give us air, fragrance, sunlight, storm. Throw word pictures of the moor on the pages of your book.'

I will do my utmost to obey you all, grateful to be commanded, proud to be your servant. Faithfully and literally I will report to you of the great moor in her varying tempers, of her humble people, of my own intimate daily life lived so joyously within the haven of her vast encircling arms.

Beatrice at the Dartmoor Window

I have chosen to begin the book today. It is Mothering Sunday and mid March. As is my custom in fine weather, I am sitting out of doors in the lily bed, working bareheaded in the sunshine. My lilies – the great, tall, strong white, dainty, fragrant, golden hearted Madonna lilies – are already five inches high and they look as lusty as a family of flourishing young cabbages. Round the corner, in the north bed, is a row of crocuses burning orange-gold against the dark earth. In a few days more, I shall pick the first daffodil. The fruitful heart of Mother Moor is already bringing forth her treasures of white and gold. In Homer Mallow Field there is another phase of motherhood. Homer Mallow...stands high above the other fields and its brown and rounded breast is covered with myriad specks of white roots broken up small for – and by – the flock. It looks as if some benevolent giant had been scattering innumerable great pearls all over the deep brown surface. Among these pearls and on them, the sheep feed with their lambs. The ewes have, until lately, been as usual in the lowlands down among Marldon among the good red earth of glorious Devon. Consequently each dame with her magnificent ruffled fleece might be an image exquisitely carved in pink coral.

The lambs are born here so they are white – pearl again, beside their coral mothers. The whole picture is flooded with pale gold sunlight and is set against a background of tors weathered in the opal-tinted veil of smoke from swaling fires whose incense rises upon every hillside.

All the moor-world today is peace and light and joyousness and rich with the incomparable treasure of Motherhood whether vegetable, animal, human or spiritual, for motherhood has many wondrous and often unsuspected phases as I have learnt since I came to dwell on the great Mother Moor.

So it is of set purpose that I have chosen to begin my book today – the great feast of motherhood – because the bringing forth of a book is one phase of spiritual motherhood. Each book is a spirit child of its author's heart and brain – a spirit child clothed in the robe of white type-embroidered paper which makes it materially visible to the eyes of all mankind."

March 14. 1915   B.C

~oOo~

In this particular book she writes of Mr Bluejacket, of the Window itself and its building, of the Rainbow Maker, Tweed Dog and the Moor in all its phases, always the moor. Of Tweed Dog (so called because her coat resembled one of Beatrice's skirts) she wrote "The beast of all beasts is the Tweed Dog who lives voluntarily by the window morning noon and night. She has worn a large patch of the bank entirely bald with her dear white pads and thumping, tweed, white-tipped tail. For years she has sat there watching me type, never barking at anyone except a sweep. The instant she sights a sweep she proceeds to kill him then and there. She always sits bolt upright holding her head rather high and if I happen to get my decorations on the window sill a little taller than is correct, she cranes over them and round them and through them till they are duly altered."

Peter Hicks on the Bank where Tweed Dog sat

The Rainbow Maker – Beatrice's mother – the name arising as a result of the chains and necklaces she made of Venetian glass of every hue from gold, rose, lilac and crystal – beads, which she sold to make money for the cottage, St Michael's Little Home of Rest for "poor gentlewomen working

11

in large cities." Three cottages stand still one side of the farmyard and in this particular one these women came to stay and were looked after by Mr Bluejacket and his wife, not even being allowed to make their own beds. Beatrice describes how the first little party arrived in May of each year.

"The poor faces that come round the corner always look the same. They are white and lined with greyish lips. A library of light reading was provided, good food, fresh air and rest, each even had their own deck chair to rest their poor backs out of doors... Each day we watched their faces getting pinker, deep lines mysteriously ironed out by magic Mother Moor...in due time their hair gets glossie and their eyes bright." It was for this the Rainbow Maker sat in the Dartmoor Window weaving rainbows – the chains and necklaces to sell to rich women in aid of their poor sisters.

The Dartmoor Window

Mrs Parr had been a social worker in the London slums and once she settled in Widecombe – apart from the cottage project – she formed a Clothing Club and a Sunday Class where she spoke – but never 'lectured' – to the farmers and their wives, and at the request of the men of the village she turned a room at St Michael's Little Home of Rest into a Working Men's Reading Room.

When she became too crippled with arthritis to turn out at night after dinner for her talks, the men assured her they would fetch her, and every evening a "Knight" arrived with a lamp to guide her while another carried her books, handed her into a chair, and took her sticks to a safe corner until she needed them again.

On wet and windy nights two more men appeared, one for extra support and one with an umbrella... "And these were the roughest boys in the place, in some cases for whom their masters had not one good word."

Mr Bluejacket shared almost equal place with Tweed Dog. "He just passed the window in his serene, unhurried way, carrying a can of water and an empty bucket. Being morning he is in working rig – the flapping wide-bottomed naval trousers, a short navy blue woollen jacket, no collar or tie, a peaked cap and clean white apron.

He is a middle aged man with silver threads in his fine, fair hair and a little flaxen moustache; he has a smart neat little short nose, the softest and kindest of blue eyes and small, well made ears. I am more sensitive about ears than I am about any other feature. He is only a common bluejacket, nothing more and nothing less, and when I begin to paint his picture in feeble words I wonder if any book is big enough to contain Mr Bluejacket."

He did everything for the two ladies from splitting logs, picking and arranging wild flowers for the dining table, to cooking and waiting at table. Vegetable growing, scrubbing floors and all the time entertaining Beatrice with tales from his long service in the navy.

It is of course impossible in a small book to give as many excerpts as I should like to try and do justice to both the writer and her writing – her description of life as it was then, of road-menders, thatchers and the prison at Princetown – read the books yourself and you will get a wonderful picture of Dartmoor in those golden years, gone forever.

One of the most fascinating of the prison, in which she took a great interest –

"I can never see that a prison is a sad object. A lunatic asylum yes, or a workhouse which shelters much helpless suffering, but a prison is surely a bracing sight. It contains only the people who deserve to be there...Prison is said to be degrading. It is not half so degrading as crime. A man has deliberately degraded himself before he reaches prison at all...our prison system in England is not degrading. It is humane and reformative before being punitive. Occasionally I visit Princetown."

Actually she took particular interest in one prisoner, visiting him many times, whose release she eventually secured. He became a member of her choir, but he died soon after and she had his grave put in the little chapel with a memorial stone in the floor.

Beatrice had a great sense of humour and she told this story about an escaped prisoner – of which there were many in those days when they worked outside on the farm and there was no means of quick communication between warder and prison as there is today with modern technology.

This is the story.

"As they mustered one afternoon to return to the prison from working outside, the warders noticed one man was missing.

They got the rest of their flock safely under lock and key and then gave the alarm. The bell was rung and a search party set out on horseback with rifles and their cartridge belts.

In about half an hour's time the 'escaped' convict arrived at the prison gates at a quick trot and in a towering passion, shouting that he wasn't going to put up with their fool tricks, and why on earth couldn't those durn idiots of warders do their work and bring a respectable convict home to his tea in a proper manner instead of leaving him at the far end of a deep ditch?

By now, he supposed his tea was cold and he would report the warders to the governor for their idiocy and carelessness." Beatrice also spent much time, between writing, looking at the passing scene from her window.

14

"The weekly butcher and the bi-weekly baker pass this way. All the farm traffic saunters under the window. Everyone who goes by is known to us. If now and then a stranger does come, think of the thrill it causes. We leave everything and gaze for it might be anyone from a distinguished convict to a bishop in mufti. Countless are the transactions performed through the Window. Orders are given to tradesman, friendly carts are pulled up on their way to the lowlands, and charged with requests to rescue a belated parcel from the station. We are one of the few villages still left in England that has no carrier of any kind.

Advice is asked as to minor ailments and salves and potions passed out and change handed in...when the hunt goes by some friend or other will deftly steer his or her horse's head in at the casement and a velvet-like nose will appear suddenly among the crockery."

And this extract from a chapter entitled A Dartmoor Day.

"The day cleared as evening came and sunset was one golden glitter that mere human eyes could hardly bear. The entire absence of wind cause a perfect stillness in every tree and bush so there was not the least movement to disturb reflection. Not a leaf is out yet so every bare wet stem was a study in wrought gold. All the fine tips and twigs were a golden lace-work, every straw of every roof had its own brilliant raindrop which reflected the sinking sun. There was not one object to be seen that was not glittering gold – exaggerated, magnified, refracted gold. After dark I was hanging out of my north bedroom window looking across to the west when I suddenly saw, sticking straight up against the dusk sky out of the dusker still hill-rim, a bright silver gold dagger blade or spear point of sword tip. Nothing was to be seen except this long sable line of hill against the lighter sky and in the highest point of the hill, this shining dagger pointing upwards. As I watched, fascinated, it slowly disappeared as if drawn downwards by some mighty unseen hand on the other side of the hill.

Strange that never in my life should I have happened to see the crescent moon set.."

Who else could have written such a magnificent, vivid description of moon set.

15

As already mentioned, animals were an important and integral part of Beatrice's life, especially Tweed Dog with whom on occasional Sundays she would take a picnic lunch on the moor.

"The wind was due north so there was not even air enough to stir a hair. The heat and light were dazzling...Tweed Dog flopped down with a groan of delight several yards off and went to sleep. Now and then she wakes, raises up her head, takes a long long look at me, vibrates her tail, drops her head, closes her eyes with an exaggerated sigh of contentment. Occasionally she rises slowly, creeps tremulous with apology to my side and approaches her muzzle very softly to my face for a kiss. She has an idea that I don't like kissing and as she cannot live without it she is intensely deprecating. As a matter of fact no one could ever tire of kissing her. She is so clean, so soft, so well bred. She smells of clean dog and new mown hay always.

She is not always a good dog I rejoice to say. At times she is uncommonly human." Beatrice gives an example of this – "The Tweed Dog, the model Dog, the essence of all that is well bred – this dog was ratting like any vulgar terrier..."

There was always a host of cats too at the house with such names as Tiger, Vim, Mike and Tinker. When they died they were buried in the field at the back of the house with stones to mark their graves.

I have a letter from George Train of Teignmouth, written to me some years ago, a man who knew her well. Here is part of his wonderful description of how Tiger became ill during one of the worst blizzards ever known on Dartmoor, and how a man risked his life to save him.

"It was during a raging blizzard on the moor with drifts 15 feet deep, telegraph poles snapped in two, ponies lying dead with ice caked on their bodies. A scene of desolation and destruction. By some miracle one telephone line was still working and Beatrice put in a frantic call to a friend of mine, an uncertified vet called Jack Saunders, but a man with a wealth of knowledge of animals acquired over the years.

In spite of his wife's pleas not to go, he left Moretonhampstead to try to reach Widecombe in an ancient Model T Ford. Having somehow struggled o within four miles of Widecombe the car gave up the ghost. He was in a poor state himself with the bitter cold and ice in the open car. He felt alone completely alone in a world bent on destroying him. He was torn between giving up and returning home, or pressing on. But he was a typical Devonshire Dumpling of yeoman stock who could not let his friend down in an hour of need.

Visibility was nil. The wind screamed like a banshee. He had left his hot drink in the car. He fell over time and time again and began to hallucinate, his limbs numb as he prayed to God for help.

He staggered on only half conscious and some lines from *"Morte d'Arthur"* by Tennyson ran through his mind – "More things are wrought by prayer than this world dreams of." And so he prayed...

When he reached Widecombe at last it was as if everyone had died. He fell into Beatrice's arms as she said 'You poor dear man, I knew you would come.'

Jack had to stay for two days and nights treating Tiger who had nearly died on the second morning, but at last the cat managed to stand up. He turned to Beatrice who had tears streaming down her face with joy, and he said 'Tiger is a born fighter, he is going to live." She replied, 'I know someone else who is a born fighter and I will never forget you.'

And indeed she wrote the whole account of his bravery in her next book.

Two other people who remembered her well were Mr and Mrs Fred Miners who now live in Ashburton. When they were first married they rented St Gabriel's Cottage next to St Michael's at the side of Venton House. At the time Fred had his own lorry for doing haulage for customers. Mrs Miners showed me a box full of postcards which Beatrice had pushed through her letterbox each morning bearing some complaint – the children or the dogs were noisy, the bonfire smoked, or Fred had disturbed her turning his lorry in the yard or under the Window. Instead of making a verbal complaint by walking a few yards she wrote it down and put the card through the letterbox a few feet from her own front door. Mrs Miners also showed me the rent book – 17/6d a week in 1949. Fred added, "She was a real character and we used to have a row over something nearly every day when I got home, but on the other hand she could be wonderfully kind i you were in trouble."

Back now to George Train. "On one occasion when I was in business the phone rang at Bovey Tracey and Beatrice's voice said urgently, 'Please listen carefully, I need your help once more..' "

There had been a blizzard similar to the one through which Jack Saunders had struggled. The moor was completely cut off, isolated and impassable This is what she told George. "There are men, women and small children desperately in need of sustenance, villages are cut off; with your business you have got equipment, tractors and so on. Go to the bakers and buy sacks of flour and loaves of bread. Please come to Buckland-in-the-Moor, that is the only road that is still open. Come as far as you can and wait. I have ar army of men digging through the drifts. They will eventually reach you and the provisions. From then on I will see to their disposal. I rely on you implicitly and know you will not fail me."

Cottages at Buckland-in-the-Moor

At the time George was working with a firm who bought and sold timber using heavy equipment, but he said when I gave the order to the drivers one of them, a tractor driver called Peter Yeo pointed out that they had families of their own to consider and it was sheer madness, suicide even to try to get through such drifts. "We'll never come back, it's an impossible situation." George simply replied "I am going – we are going – okay?"

And so the little calvacade set off from the silent town, climbing the hill to Buckland-in-the-Moor from where they could go no further. They had fought their way through what could only be described as a titanic blizzard. Now they stood waiting, almost frozen to the ground, slapping their arms to keep the circulation going, straining their ears for a sound of the men coming to meet them, and at last, as Beatrice had promised, the exhausted men appeared, struggling through the mountainous drifts, panting with the exertion of digging.

Gratefully they took the sacks of food and fuel.

Some time after Beatrice wrote a book, *"The Ghost of the Moor"*, a copy of which she sent to George. In it she swore that but for the kindness and generosity and courage of George Train and his men there would have been many more ghosts on the moor.

Commandment Stones at Buckland-in-the-Moor

George ended his letter to me.. "These are a few of the stories about a lady who I feel sure in the Heavenly Mansions has reaped her reward. By some she was misjudged and ill treated for she had fallen by the wayside, and the Pharisees passed her by."

19

Sadly George died aged 90 some years ago, but I went to see his wif
and she told me she remembered Beatrice well.

"Cobwebs and seed cake! Ill never forget going to Venton House. Yo
had to fight your way through the cobwebs. This was in 1954, not lon
before she died. George used to bring her back home for a meal and sh
always asked for seed cake which was one of her favourites."

Mrs Train was a midwife and district nurse in the area and remembers th
trip made from Bovey Tracey to Buckland-in-the-Moor. "He worked wit
Heaths who were timber merchants and had heavy vehicles such as tractors
Once George had persuaded them to go they rushed round the town gettin
sacks of flour and potatoes to do as Beatrice asked. George thought th
world of her, he had met her at Venton when he went to that area to bu
timber."

Undoubtedly one of the people who knew Beatrice better than anyon
else is Miss Enid Shortbridge. Her father was a doctor in South Africa fo
some years before he returned to a practice in Honiton. Enid had bee
homesick in Africa and quite by chance she found a book entitled *"Th
Heart of the Moor"* by Beatrice Chase. Enid had only visited Dartmoo
once but it had fascinated her and she was determined that when the
eventually returned to England she must meet the author. However someon
told her Beatrice was dead, that was in 1922, but on returning to England i
1924 she found out that of course this was not true, Beatrice was still ver
much alive.

Enid wrote to the publisher asking for Beatrice's address. She said, "
had a shock when I found out her name was not Beatrice Chase at all bu
Katharine Parr. That was only the first of many shocks. I expected the Lad
of the Moor to be tall, elegant graceful. Actually she was quite stocky
about 5 feet 6 inches tall. It's hard to describe her as a person if you don'
know her. Even then you would never have known the real Beatrice. People
had no half measures over their feelings, they either liked her or disliked he
intensely. My own first meeting was not good.

I travelled down to Widecombe and my bus was late getting to Venton
This apparition stuck her head out of an upstairs window and said "You ar

Beatrice at Poet's Corner

late. I cannot see you at this time. You will have to stay overnight. There's nowhere in Widecombe. You will have to try either Bovey Tracey or Ashburton."

I did manage to find somewhere in Ashburton and came back the next morning, I was not looking forwards at all to the meeting. She was in her little chapel. A different person. All sweetness and light, the most gracious, charming lady you could imagine and I had a wonderful day with her.

That was Beatrice, you could never tell from one minute to the next how her mood would be – she was the ultimate person of moods.

I think her greatest attraction was a beautiful speaking voice which John Oxenham described as having a 'flute-like tone.' Her hair was a yellow shade and when it went grey she dyed it henna red. She was always muffled up to the neck, majestic, Victorian. We were close, very close friends for 30 years. She had many friends but used regularly to fall out with them.

As a matter of fact no one really knew her, she was an enigma. Remember the Greek myth of Echo and Narcissus? He fell in love with his reflection – Katharine Parr created the image of Beatrice Chase and then fell in love with it. In all her books she is the heroine. I really wish people would let her rest because it is so difficult to get at the real person. She was a strangely complex character, absurdly naive for a woman of her age, and an incurable romantic living in a dream world in which she saw herself as a mixture of priestess and one of King Arthur's Court, but in a twisted sort of way. She adored men but not in a sexual way, They were little tin gods on pedestals and women were very much second-class citizens. One of her favourite sayings was 'All women are sad or mad or both!'

She was sensual but not towards humans, and this was probably at the root of much of her mental confusion at the last. I often wonder what a psycho-analyst would have made of her. I met several of the characters in the various local stories – and they were not quite as described (a poet in his own country!)

I played a trick on her once. She did have a sense of humour but liked to be the one who made the jokes without too much competition!

This is what I did – when they opened Exeter airport I knew several of the young pilots and I thought it would be fun to fly over Widecombe and

Venton where they'd never seen a plane before. I rang Beatrice and told her a huge bird was coming to sit on her roof, then I sent a telegram signing it as though it had come from the Duchess of Bedford, at the time a well known, eccentric pilot. Then that afternoon some friends and I flew over Venton. Next day, 23 May 1935 she wrote to me..."Yesterday at 4.30 my calm was suddenly shattered by a telegram 'Hoping to pay you an aerial visit today about 6.15. Plane green with silver wings and a number.' While I was taking this down over the phone my thoughts flew to you but the signature was the Duchess of Bedford...I set my phone merrily ringing for twenty minutes or so and told everyone what was happening. She arrived at quarter to six. Majestic, stately, ducal. I felt sick with excitement to see her. She circled three times slowly round Venton and then sailed away. She did not perch on the roof and preen her wings or turn upside down and hang head downwards or any of your stunts. Golly, how you scared me! Your loving old friend Beatrice."

Enid continued – " I was the last person but one to see her before she died. I was with her in the afternoon, she died at 8 o'clock. It was a pathetic death and I think if her enemies could have seen her at the last they would have forgiven her.

The irony was that although she died of cancer she had never smoked, it was the various Bluejackets she employed as her servants who smoked all the time. If only smokers could see the damage they do to people. You couldn't help being sorry for her, she was like a child, not really responsible.."

Another character who knew her well is Peter Hicks, not only a retired farmer but the man who plays Uncle Tom Cobley at Widecombe Fair, whose face is known in snapshots, photos and videos all over the world taken by the thousands of visitors to the Fair each summer.

His father and mother ran the farm at Venton in Beatrice's day, Peter was in his late 'teens and remembers how she became a recluse, probably due to the cancer from which she was suffering.

"I was the only person she eventually allowed in the house, I would take her a cup of tea – I was the only one too who knew where she kept her loaded revolver.

She was an eccentric lady, one day she would tell me I would benefit greatly in her will, then like a sudden change in the weather, the next day she would pick some reason for leaving me out. But when she died she left me Venton, although there was a heavy mortgage."

He showed me over the house with its different named rooms, and into the tiny chapel, sadly empty now of all its glory, except for the magnificent stained glass windows she had had made by hand, no expense spared.

Peter pointed to a window on the ground floor of the extension Beatrice and her mother had had built on, "That's the famous Dartmoor Window where she sat to write, and outside on the bank is where Tweed Dog sat.."

Peter Hicks in his favourite corner at Venton

Cats' Memorial Stone

We went into the field where her beloved cats are buried with headstones still standing, where she had wanted to be buried. He showed me the well with its pump above the spring which she had got men to dig down for, having said she had seen it in a vision. Peter went on, "She was certainly a remarkable woman, a brilliant person who could have been a King's Councillor if she wished. She was temperamental, but wonderfully kind – if she liked you! She had such a sad end."

At the side of the yard, near the house, stand the cottages, St Gabriel's where Fred Miners and his wife lived, St Michael's where the working women from the city came for their holidays, and beyond them the house where the faithful Mr Bluejackets and their wives lived in turn.

Beatrice wrote much about the ghosts of the Moor, the legends and folklore, she said, "I maintain that things do not happen in other places as they happen here. Sudden deaths upon the moor or the highway are frequent, deaths apparently with insufficient cause." The most famous of her books on this subject is *"The Corpse on the Moor"* telling of the strange death of a man at Postbridge, a case which was never resolved.

Tinker's Grave

She wrote of the famous Coffin Stone, the large flat stone halfway down the hill into Widecombe where for hundreds of years coffins in transit were rested. The stone is cleft through in the centre and an old legend says that years ago when the coffin of a wicked man was resting on the stone, a flash of lightning struck it and cleft the boulder in twain. She goes on to bewail thus – "...the horsedrawn hearse is destroying the beautiful old moorland

26

custom of hand carried coffins. Some people still cling to the old way by which a pole is passed through two rings at the head and foot of the coffin, enabling it to be carried many miles over any kind of country by simply changing bearers from time to time."

She tells of a man who committed suicide by shooting himself upon the open moor and fell dead exactly at the boundary of two parishes, his shattered head in one parish and his body in the other, resulting in a discussion as to which parish should be responsible for his burial.

She was the first person to put flowers on the grave of Mary Jay, an orphan apprentice from Newton Abbot Workhouse about the same period when Dickens was writing of Oliver Twist. Her name is on the Apprentices' Register long discarded, at the age of 15 she was apprenticed to a farmer near Wingstone and in due course took a rope and hanged herself in a barn.

Jay's Grave

In those days they would not bury suicides in consecrated ground so she was dumped at the wayside and forgotten. Her grave was unmarked until Squire Bryant of Hedgebarton found it in about 1850 and he had the skeleton put in a box and raised the pathetic little grass mound where several parishes meet. Her employer's son had made her pregnant without any hope of marriage and in those days the world did not look kindly on one parent families, specially in such an isolated and close knit community. Since then fresh flowers appear regularly on the grave all year round and in spite of the efforts of many different people, no one has ever been seen actually placing them there.

Beatrice also located the Broadstone below Rowbrook Farm where the River Dart makes that incredible moaning sound which I heard myself when I went to talk to the late Algy May at the farm and he told me the story of Jan Coo, the young farm apprentice who had heard it too, and the sound of his name wafted on the breeze so he ran out of the farm one summer evening, drawn, compelled by the voice, down to the river, never to be seen again.

Beatrice also helped to revive interest in Widecombe Fair which had become little more than a sheep sale in the 1930s. She sent a telegram to the BBC on the morning of the Fair (in those days the orange envelope arrived at its destination within hours – not days). She asked them to include the song about Uncle Tom Cobley on the 10 o'clock news slot to tell people it was Fair Day. As a result the biggest crowd the village had ever seen flocked to the green and the field where the main part of the fair was to be held, and since then the day has been an overwhelming success and part of the Devon scene.

To return to her sense of humour – she said that although sitting in her Dartmoor Window and writing was pure ecstasy, like most writers she had trouble with her various typewriters, one of which would put in letters she had not asked for. This particular machine was known as the Demon of the Dartmoor Window, for instance "Dear Mr Smith" became "Deaf Mr Smith" and when ordering a chicken from the butcher it wrote "A fine fat fool dressed ready for the oven."

She spoke her mind always, sometimes without much tact, and when I was giving a talk in Ashburton some of the ladies in the audience told me they remembered her well as she went to their church on occasions where she had a pew reserved, and woebetide anyone who might take it by mistake, she did not hesitate to hit them smartly on the shoulder with her walking stick.

She was a trend setter, a character and personality without being a pale copy of others, a disease which seems to assail so many today. At one time she was due to appear at Ashburton Petty Sessions Court on a criminal libel charge on information which had been lodged by the Abbot of Buckfast, but the case collapsed on retraction and an apology.

Beatrice in Land Girls outfit

29

She was also firm and dogmatic if she got an idea into her head as in the incident already mentioned, of the well. When she had first gone to Venton she knew the name was Celtic for spring and was certain one must exist and was proved right although the locals assured her there had been no sign of such a thing in living memory, but she still insisted they dig and was proved right.

Her faith was even more important to her than her work, and when her fiancé had been killed she had once thought of entering the Dominican Order. Her little chapel was granted full privileges to restore mass and the Reservation to the old world village which had once been a Catholic stronghold. However after taking her noviciate vows she took the matter no further, although after the Privilege of the Reservation of the Blessed Sacrament was given to her she vowed never to leave Venton for one night while it was present, and for this she wore a gold chain on her left hand to indicate she was chained or wedded to Dartmoor and the Blessed Sacrament.

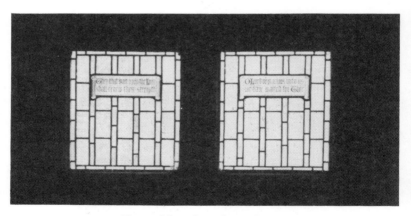

Two of the chapel windows

In those days the chapel had plain white walls and stained glass windows made to her design by hand. They are all that still remains of the former glory. A lamp with a ruby red glass burned outside the door which was always open to passers-by.

Pump and well

It was really before and during the First World War that her fame spread so widely when she kept a Roll of Honour with the names of the White Crusaders or Knights. People considered her to be their leader and men in the trenches, their wives and sweethearts all wrote to Venton house pledging to be true to Honour, and in return she prayed for their souls in the little chapel. There, among so many souvenirs, she had a Military Cross and DSO sent to her from a man who had returned safely from the Battle of Vimy Ridge, convinced his safety was due to her prayers. During the summer months in those far off '20s and '30s over 300 people used to visit

31

the little chapel, or if they could not come in person, they sent a telegram asking her to pray for sick friends.

Perhaps in all fairness by today's standards she would not have been in the top echelon of writers for her books, particularly her fiction, are written in very flowery language and extremely sentimental unlike such contemporary writers of romantic fiction as Joanna Trollope. Although some of her love scenes could compare with Mills and Boon or Barbara Cartland – and none the worse for that for there is a reader for every kind of writing, and there is no doubt she brought enormous pleasure to people from all over the world.

As already stated, many of her books were destroyed during the war as she wrote in her book *'The Dartmoor Window Forty Years After.'* "All those faithful servants are now dead...the men who were memorised in my *'Dartmoor Window'* books, now out of print, the last of which were wiped out when the Hun destroyed Paternoster Row and Ludgate on 29 December 1940. Over eight million books went that awful night and for eight empty, barren, idle years have my humble creative powers and active brain been growing stagnant moss, only two books have appeared in that long period."

This was when she published her own books in paperback form.

"So now, incredible as it seems, I am back once more in my own literary kingdom and able to give you news from my Dartmoor Window. As usual the poor publishers are handicapped by lack of paper, the expense of cloth binding etc. so I am publishing myself as soon as possible with a stiff paper cover...and am intending to send you news gathered since 1918 and published largely in Chambers Journals, Edinburgh, whose editor has kindly given me permission for reproduction."

In 1946 *"The Corpse on the Moor"* had been published in this way by S T Elson of Ashburton, *"The Dartmoor Window Forty Years On"* in November 1948, *"Dartmoor the Beloved"* in August 1951. In these two latter many identical chapters are contained but in the "Forty Years On" edition she states how she started the Uncle Tom Cobley (sic) procession by presenting a genuine smock frock from Norfolk to Mr Dunn, which gave him the idea of impersonating that famous gentleman and now (1948) his son Mr Albert Dunn carries on the tradition.

It is interesting that in the 1951 edition of *"Dartmoor The Beloved"* the name of the author is given as Katharine Parr with Beatrice Chase in brackets underneath. Was she for the moment returning to her basic self or did she half fear the public might have forgotten her dual personality? Could it be her alto ego taking over, had she run out of steam? It does happen to many writers.

Perhaps she felt the nine chapters repeated in the second book are among the best she had written. Some of the others are admittedly a hotch potch away from her beloved moor with tales of Ike Eisenhower to whom she reported that his troops stationed on Dartmoor during the war (many at Cherrybrook Powder Mills) were killing the wild birds. Ike wrote back saying he had given orders that no bird was to be touched, and his orders were obeyed.

Colonel Fawcett, the explorer, who disappeared in South America had been warned by Beatrice whom he came to see. She told him not to make this last journey, she knew he would fail. And he did. It was while he was living at Seaton that he called on her. He was one of the leading members on the Crusade of the White Knights which she had formed with John Oxenham.

Cats of course are everywhere in the book including Ike and Sandy, marmalade cats. By now Tweed Dog had died, but there was to be no mourning as she was convinced of a future existence for animals.

Cranmere Pool was always a subject she could not resist and she wrote in both books about the post box founded there by the famous moorland guide, Mr Sandford Perrott of Chagford. It had been removed for safety during the war and there was a formal ceremony performed by Mrs St Leger Gordon to replace it in its original spot.

Among her many interests she was a member of the Royal Meteorological Society for whom she kept records and in 1951 she describes that wonderful sight – the Ammil.

"Twigs, blades of grass and stalks are coated with a clear ice so that the wind in the hedges makes music like silver bells and yet the roads are not affected. A Dartmoor phenomenon when ice covers all it can find giving the moor a white, enamelled shine."

There is also in this book a list of "Peeves" – perhaps a hint of the bitterness to come. Here are just a few –

"Why do all press pictures of women show a shark like grin extending even to their back teeth?

Why do they paint their nails in a hideous blood red spoiling the delicate pink colours and white half-moon of the natural nail?

Why do they cut a hole in their toes to show a big toe nail also dyed red?

Why do all novelists say 'He rose to his feet' and 'he nodded his head.' What else can you rise to or nod?

If girls don't like being battered and murdered why do they drink in pubs with strange men and then go with them down dark lanes?"

She was a staunch defender of keeping the moor as it was, with a bitter hatred of the National Parks Bill. On All Saints Day 1951 when the decision to keep Dartmoor a National Park had stood, she wrote – "The whole of England and the big open spaces, the watersheds and visibility from the sea for signalling are being seized...for our enemies. That is the plain truth."

I wonder what she would have thought of the channel tunnel.

Beatrice's bedroom today

Let us end these quotes with some description so typical of her writing at its best, taken from these two booklets.

"Winter days on Dartmoor – Rising at 6.30 by candlelight and lamplight– breakfast at 7.30, the odours of toast, eggs and bacon, coffee, the glories of the sun rising behind tors – black, rose, gold, grey, and great ranges of snow clouds sweeping out over the great moor. Exercise in ski-ing suit, walking till tea time, a blazing log fire in the open fireplace, dinner of squab pie, plum pudding, stilton cheese and fruit. Books, needlework, letters and games.

Sometimes I throw on a fur coat just before bed time and go out to look at the snow clad moor.

On moonlight nights I wrap up in a padded cloak and sit in a deck chair under a high hedge in the garden and listen to the north wind thunder in the bare branches of the sycamores, and the whispers and chuckles of the dead leaves as they scurry across the grass murmuring to each other of the flirtation of the past dead summer.

Every rhododendron bush is a tangle of shimmering silver and throws India ink shadows on the bare earth below. The night wind is cold, clear and fragrant as iced cider cup and there is not a cloud from horizon to horizon. The moon rides high and unattended except for her courtier stars."

In 1930 she suddenly launched into a new career by taking up photography with a simple Brownie Box camera, a very popular model in those days. She became so expert with her Dartmoor scenes, views and people, that Ralph Tuck, the famous postcard producer, signed her up to work for him. As she was a great walker, rambling over her beloved moor, she was an ideal person to take pictures of so many places – unknown to many people – such as Bonehill, Bellever, even Cranmere, and the men of the moor at work, peat cutting, thatching, ploughing, hay making – going about their daily tasks.

But the clouds were starting to gather and she wrote to a friend "Times are bad and the photography stunt is as the last plan to the shipwrecked." This was when she decided to sell her books and photos from her own house and in 1931 she published a book of *"Dartmoor Snapshots"*, a record of a way of life gone forever.

By now her fame had become tiresome to her, demands by the public were turning sour, she was acquiring a reputation for bitterness, visitors overwhelmed her, interfering with her privacy and her writing.

She put up notices couched in curt terms such as FASTEN THE GATE.. ..CHAPEL CLOSED – such behaviour unheard of in the past. She was a victim of her own fame, today perhaps we would call it a Catch 22 situation.

Beatrice's Mother's Grave

In the 1940s the horrors of war prompted her to try to revive her Purity Crusade, but the people of the Second World War would have none of it. The public had already forgotten her. She was alone and no longer loved or respected.

Such is the fickleness of the world...

Beatrice had channelled all her energy and money into a campaign to stop the use of Dartmoor for military training and in opposition to the Establishment – of making the moor a National Park. Most likely if the phrase had been invented then she would have quoted Dartmoor as the 'Last Wilderness' and that as such it should be preserved, a sentiment with which many people identify today.

She sold her jewellery and her library, the few friends she had left were offered copies of her books at half price, but now there was hardly any demand for her work.

The warm side of her nature was crushed and she became bitter and spiteful. As Peter said, she kept a loaded gun at her side and would open the door to no one but him.

Before that in 1953 or '54 George Train still managed to see her in spite of the foreboding notices, but now she had no servant, only what she called her "blimming telephone" which always seemed to be out of order and on which she made up to 90 calls a day when she could, telephoning doctors, neighbours, the police and solicitors. She had tried to communicate with people who had outgrown her way of life, in fact the world itself had outgrown her fervent type of faith.

The ever faithful George drove her round the moor, taking her to the places she knew and loved so well, of which she had written; finally he would take her back to his own home for a good meal as it was obvious she was not eating properly. Once, with a flash of her old humour she said "Anyone can write a book, it takes an expert to cook a really good meal."

At last she became so ill she had to be taken to Newton Abbot Infirmary under the terms of the National Assistance Act – a person who needed care and attention. She died there on Sunday night 3rd July 1955, two days before her eighty-first birthday. She had asked to be buried in the field near her beloved animals' graves behind the house where she had lived for 50 years, in a coffin with no lid and dressed in her Dominican habit. However her grave is in Widecombe churchyard opposite that of her mother, and she was clothed in her Dominican habit.

She left the farm to Peter "in recognition of his unfailing helpfulness," but it was heavily mortgaged. Her authors first copies of all her books she left to the Holy Child Convent in Cavendish Square and the manuscripts to the RSPCA. The total net cash she then had was £2,019.

The memorial stone bears the inscription "PRAY FOR OLIVE KATHARINE PARR" and on the other side "Beatrice Chase 1874-1955." This was paid for by a small committee which had been formed at the suggestion of her great friend, Enid Shortbridge and consisted of Jan Stewer, Hamlyn Parsons and Lois Deacon who had written a book about Mary Jay.

Beatrice's Grave

Beatrice's death went almost unnoticed in the literary world. Had she died at the zenith of her success she would have been mourned world wide. The only national press reference I could find was in the News Chronicle written two days after her death with the heading "Lady of the Moor Kept a Gun." Such was her epitaph. They also stated that her house had figured in an Anthony Asquith film *"A Cottage on Dartmoor"*.

However many people do still remember her and read her books and poetry with pleasure for she left us some of the most beautiful and vivid descriptions of Dartmoor, and time has softened the memory of the bitter, lonely old woman with her cruel tongue; this was not the same person who had written of the beauty and goodness which had made her famous in a golden world, gone forever.

The bank where Tweed Dog sat is still there below the window that looked across the moor, although the hedge has grown up now to hide the view. The chapel is neglected and used as a store. A century has passed since she was born but Venton House still stands, surely full of the ghosts of Beatrice, The Rainbow Maker, Tiger, Tweed Dog and the various Mr Bluejackets, for all of whom life must have been much like an evening in May, and I feel that the words from that now famous poem written by an unknown soldier killed in battle, could not ring more truly for anyone than the Beatrice Chase who was My Lady of the Moor, who so loved nature and the passing seasons, so let us leave her with an excerpt which would have made a perfect epitaph.

>   " I am the thousand winds that blow,
>   I am the diamond glints on snow,
>   I am the sunlight on the ripened grain,
>   I am the gentle autumn rain
>   As you wake with morning's hush,
>   I am the swift up flinging rush
>   Of quiet birds in circling flight,
>   I am the day transcending light.. "